Developing
Professional Skills:
Constitutional Law

Brannon P. Denning
Professor
Cumberland School of Law
Samford University

Colleen Medill
Series Editor

WEST
ACADEMIC
PUBLISHING

© 2014 LEG, Inc. d/b/a West Academic
444 Cedar Street, Suite 700
St. Paul, MN 55101
1-877-888-1330

West, West Academic Publishing, and West Academic are trademarks of West Publishing Corporation, used under license.

Printed in the United States of America

MAT#41513950
ISBN: 978-0-314-28974-2

This book is dedicated to my students, past and future.

Preface

LAW SCHOOLS TODAY aspire to teach professional legal skills. The current emphasis on skills training is in response to the criticism that the traditional law school curriculum does not adequately train students to practice law. The high cost of law school tuition, coupled with the tight job market for law school graduates in recent years, has intensified the demand for more skills training in law schools.

Incorporating skills training into doctrinal law courses is challenging. Elaborate simulations can crowd out the coverage of fundamental legal concepts and doctrines, leaving both the professor and the students frustrated. The professor feels that there is never enough time to cover the subject matter adequately. The students feel that there is never enough time, period.

Developing Professional Skills: Constitutional Law is designed to provide skills training to law students in a time-efficient manner. Each chapter in this book focuses on one of the following four core legal skills:

▶ Client Counseling (including engagement of a new client, interviewing and fact gathering);

▶ Legal Drafting (including client correspondence via letters and e-mails as well as traditional legal document drafting);

▶ Negotiation; and

▶ Advocacy.

Students are expected to spend about one to two hours outside of the classroom preparing the skills assignment for each chapter. A comprehensive Teacher's Manual gives the professor both guidance and discretion in determining how much classroom discussion time to devote to the material in each chapter. The professor may spend a brief amount of time reviewing the "answer" to the problem presented in the chapter. Or, the professor may expand the discussion to include concepts of professional responsibility and the norms of modern legal practice. Suggestions for incorporating professional responsibility concepts and the norms of legal practice into the classroom discussion are contained in the Teacher's Manual. For professors who desire to expand the scope of a skills exercise, selected provisions of the Model Rules of Professional Conduct and client time sheets are reproduced as Appendix material at the end of the book.

Developing Professional Skills: Constitutional Law is intended to bring to life the materials taught in the basic Constitutional Law course. The standard classroom routine of reading cases and answering questions generally is not what students envision when they enter law school. As lawyers, students will encounter idiosyncratic, demanding, and occasionally unreasonable clients, constantly evolving new technology, old-fashioned financial and time management constraints, and most of all, interesting problems to solve. Importantly, they will then be asked to implement their solutions to those problems. Although no book can truly simulate the nuanced tapestry that is modern legal practice, the skills exercises in this book can be used to enhance and enrich the students' educational experience and lead them a significant step closer to being practicing lawyers and legal counselors.

Several generous friends provided support and willingly shared their expertise to assist me in the writing of this book. First and foremost, I thank Colleen Medill, Warren R. Wise Professor of Law at the University of Nebraska and the creator and primary force behind the Developing Professional Skills series, for her support, encouragement and invitation to participate in this important project.

I also thank Staci Herr, Senior Acquisitions Editor at West Academic Publishing and Louis Higgins, who is West Academic's Editor-in-Chief, for the opportunity to contribute to this series. Dean John Carroll and the Cumberland School of Law provided financial support for this project, for which I am grateful. I also want to thank my constitutional law students who unknowingly field tested many of the problems that found their way into this volume.

Brannon P. Denning
April, 2014

Introduction

Developing Professional Skills: Constitutional Law introduces you to the variety of skills that differentiate the law student from the experienced legal practitioner. Like any type of skill, acquiring professional legal skills takes time and patience, but most of all, it takes practice. Each chapter in this book provides you with the opportunity to practice a legal skill that you are likely to use again and again after you graduate from law school.

The chapters of this book are organized according to topics that usually are covered in the basic Constitutional Law course. In Chapter One, you are offering an opinion on the constitutionality of proposed legislation to a non-lawyer journalist. In Chapter Two, you are drafting a brief on behalf of the United States government to accompany a motion to dismiss a suit by members of Congress upset over the certification of a constitutional amendment. Chapter Three finds you advising a corporate client on the prospects of a constitutional challenge to proposed legislation that threatens to subject his business to heavy taxation. Chapter Four involves both an evaluation of the constitutionality of an ordinance drafted by your client, the town council. The exercise also invites you to alter the draft ordinance, if necessary, to insulate it from legal challenge. In Chapter Five you assume the role of a lawyer with the Office of Legal Counsel, the constitutional lawyers of the executive branch. The President is trying to make up his mind about an issue and wants to read opposing views. Your boss instructs you to draft a memo arguing that a particular piece of legislation is unconstitutional. Your task in Chapter Six is to negotiate on behalf of a sitting governor with members of the legislature in an attempt to water down legislation that the governor fears will enmesh the state in costly litigation. Chapter Seven asks you to counsel your client, a state university, on how it might lawfully consider race in its undergraduate admissions process. In Chapter Eight, you are asked to respond to the indictment of a client's son for suspected terroristic threatening and incitement to commit murder. Chapter Nine finds you advising your client, a local school system, whether a principal's discipline of a student violated the student's First Amendment rights, leaving the school system vulnerable to a lawsuit. In Chapter Ten you are instructed to negotiate over the content of a courthouse display that contains religious texts and iconography.

Client counseling, legal drafting, negotiation, and advocacy are the core skills of the legal profession. *Developing Professional Skills: Constitutional Law* provides you with an opportunity to begin acquiring these skills.

Table of Contents

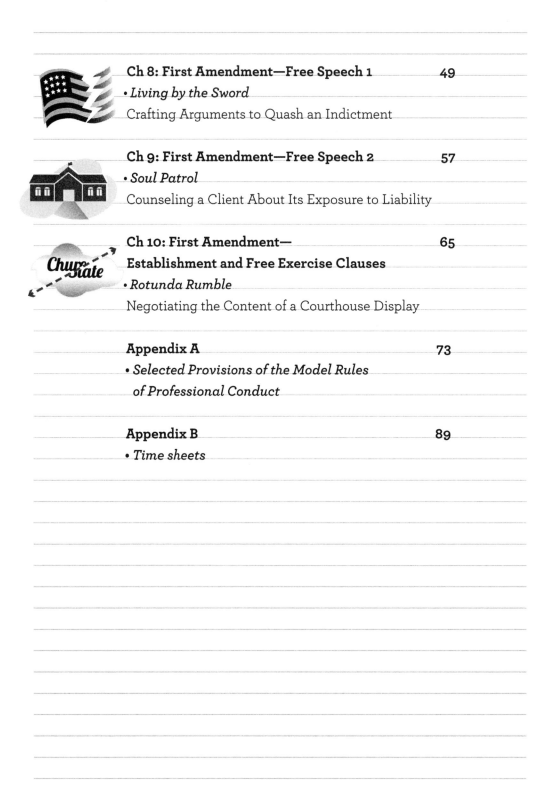

Developing Professional Skills:
CONSTITUTIONAL LAW

CHAPTER ONE

Judicial Review and Congressional Control of Jurisdiction
Pledging Allegiance

IT'S MONDAY MORNING when the phone rings at your firm. You pick up the phone and recognize the voice of your old undergraduate classmate, Frieda Cohn, now an editor for a national paper.

"Do you have a minute?" she asked.

"For you, Frieda," you respond, "I've got five!"

"Such a card. Okay smartie, have you seen this bill that seeks to prevent federal courts from reviewing challenges to the use of 'under God' in the Pledge of Allegiance?"

"Uh, no," you respond, "I'm not surprised, though. Every time that a court renders an unpopular decision, Congress stands ready to strip the courts of jurisdiction."

"Okay, we want to run an editorial opposing the bill—saying that it's probably unconstitutional, it is isn't it?— but we wanted to talk to someone who knows something about law, so we don't look stupid. I knew

> you were a lawyer, so here I am calling. Can you explain to us in three pages or less whether and why this bill is unconstitutional?"
>
> "Uh Frieda," you begin to explain, "I'm not really what you would call a constitutional law expert. I put together municipal bond deals."
>
> "Oh, pleeeese. C'mon, we want to run this thing soon; I'll throw in a free subscription! Anyway, bonds, shmonds, I know you're interested in all that constitutional stuff. Look, I'm emailing you a copy of the law. Just give us your opinion, and remember, you're writing for a bunch of non-lawyers, okay? Great. I owe you one."

Sighing, you hang up. *I don't have time for this! Why do I let her talk me into these things?* You're still grumbling as you open her email containing the text of the following bill.

To: Eager Young Associate [eya@bigfirm.com]
From: Frieda Cohn [friedac@bigcitytimes.com]
Re: Pledge of Allegiance Bill
📎: senateBill.docx

Thanks a ton for looking this over!
You're the best! Let me know what you think,

—Frieda

IN THE SENATE OF THE UNITED STATES
January 4, 20__

A BILL

To amend title 28, United States Code, with respect to the jurisdiction of Federal courts over certain cases and controversies involving the Pledge of Allegiance.

Be it enacted by the Senate and House of Representatives of the United States of America in Congress assembled,

SECTION 1. SHORT TITLE.

This Act may be cited as the 'Pledge Protection Act'.

SEC. 2. LIMITATION ON JURISDICTION.

Chapter 99 of title 28, United States Code, is amended by adding at the end the following:

'Sec. 1632. Limitation on jurisdiction

'No court created by Act of Congress shall have any jurisdiction, and the Supreme Court shall have no appellate jurisdiction, to hear or decide any question pertaining to the interpretation of, or the validity under the Constitution of, this section or the Pledge of Allegiance, as defined in section 4 of title 4, or its recitation.'

Points to Consider:

(1) What, precisely, does § 1632 *do*? Does it do more than one thing?

(2) What is the practical *effect* of § 1632? Does it foreclose *all* legal challenges to the use of "under God" in the Pledge?
    No; can go to state ct,

(3) What is the strongest argument *in favor* of the Act's constitutionality? The strongest *against*?

(4) You admitted to Frieda that you are not a constitutional law expert. Even if you are willing, can you ethically opine as to the Act's constitutionality when the issue is outside of your practice area?

(5) Would agreeing to provide legal advice on this issue for the paper preclude your firm from representing a future client against the paper, even on an unrelated matter, in the future? Is there anything you might do to ensure that your firm is not excluded from, say, representing a union in a future labor dispute with Frieda's paper?

Client Counseling Memo

Your Name:

Client's Name:

Date:

Client Goals:

Key Points Regarding Consitutionality of § 1632:

   In favor:

   Against:

Potential Conflicts:

Recommendations:

CHAPTER TWO

Standing and Justiciability
Balancing Act

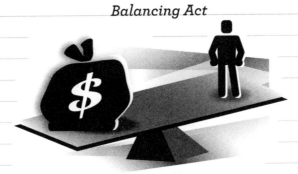

IN REACTION TO what was seen as irresponsible spending by the U.S. Congress, momentum built to amend the U.S. Constitution to include a Balanced Budget Amendment ("BBA"). In relevant part, what would become the Twenty-eighth Amendment read that "[t]otal outlays for any fiscal year shall not exceed total receipts for that fiscal year, unless three-fifths of the whole number of each House of Congress shall provide by law for a specific excess of outlays over receipts by a roll call vote." Other provisions of the BBA prohibited increasing the amount of government debt held by the public without a three-fifths supermajority, and required the President to present Congress with a balanced budget prior to the start of each fiscal year.

As required by Article V of the U.S. Constitution (which is reprinted in its entirety at the end) the BBA received the requisite two-thirds votes of both houses of Congress. Congress then submitted the BBA to the states for ratification by state legislatures. (The President has no role in the amendment process, so proposed amendments are not submitted for his signature or veto.) The Constitution requires that three-quarters of state legislatures ratify the amendment; the affirmative votes of thirty-eight states were needed for the BBA to become part of the Constitution.

According to the U.S. Code, the Archivist of the United States decides when that threshold has been crossed. When the Archivist receives official notice at the National Archives and Records Administration "that any amendment proposed to the Constitution of the United States has been adopted, according to the provisions of the Constitution," the Archivist "shall . . . cause the amendment to be published, with his certificate, specifying the States by which the [amendment] may have been adopted, and that the [amendment] has become valid . . . as a part of the Constitution of the United States." 1 U.S.C. § 106b.

Initially, the amendment enjoyed easy success in the states, as memories of profligate spending leading to runaway deficits and higher taxes lingered. But as the BBA approached the number of states needed for ratification, some states experienced second thoughts. Following state elections, Arizona and Nevada both voted to rescind their prior ratification of the BBA. Fears expressed by the BBA's opponents who now controlled the legislatures of both states—that the BBA's passage would empower courts to force spending cuts and even to raise taxes—proved persuasive. With Arizona and Nevada now both voting "no," the number of states voting to ratify fell from thirty-seven to thirty-five. The original proponents of the BBA in those states, however, as well as the congressional delegations from both states, whose members favor the amendment, take the position that the rescissions were ineffective and that only one more state legislature needed to ratify the BBA for it to become effective.

A few weeks later, New Mexico voted to ratify the BBA, which put the number of ratifying states at either thirty-eight or thirty-six, depending on whether Arizona and Nevada's rescissions were valid. As the debate was raging, the Archivist of the United States published the BBA as the new Twenty-eighth Amendment to the Constitution and certified that it had been validly adopted and was a part of the Constitution. His certificate listed Arizona and Nevada as having ratified the BBA; it made no mention of their alleged rescissions.

Furious, members of the legislatures in Arizona and Nevada who
voted to rescind their states' early ratification filed suit in federal court
seeking to enjoin the enforcement of the Amendment and an order
requiring the Archivist *decertify* the BBA.

On behalf of the Archivist of the United States, the Department of
Justice is opposing the legislators' suits. Your boss, the Attorney
General, has asked you to draft part of a brief to be filed in support
of a motion to dismiss the lawsuit that contests both (1) the standing
of the legislators to bring suit and (2) the justiciability of the
Archivist's actions.

* * *

Article V of the U.S. Constitution reads:

> *The Congress, whenever two thirds of both houses shall
> deem it necessary, shall propose amendments to this
> Constitution, or, on the application of the legislatures of
> two thirds of the several states, shall call a convention for
> proposing amendments, which, in either case, shall be
> valid to all intents and purposes, as part of this
> Constitution, when ratified by the legislatures of three
> fourths of the several states, or by conventions in three
> fourths thereof, as the one or the other mode of ratifica-
> tion may be proposed by the Congress; provided that
> no amendment which may be made prior to the year one
> thousand eight hundred and eight shall in any manner
> affect the first and fourth clauses in the ninth section of
> the first article; and that no state, without its consent, shall
> be deprived of its equal suffrage in the Senate.*

Points to Consider:

(1) Do legislators have any special status that relaxes the constitutionally-mandated standing requirements, as articulated by the Supreme Court?

(2) Can the state legislators claim any particular "injury" that isn't widely shared?

(3) Does either Article V or the relevant statute provide for a judicial role in the amendment process?

(4) Article V is silent on the efficacy of rescissions. Does this fact cut in favor of or against the state legislators?

(5) After you complete your assignment, you leave the Department of Justice for private practice. You join your new firm's Chicago office. Upon arrival you find that, lo and behold, lawyers in the firm's Phoenix office are representing the state legislators in the litigation against the Archivist. Can you assist them in their case? May the firm continue to represent the legislators now that you have joined? What steps might the firm take to keep the lawyers (and the firm) from being disqualified from representing the legislators?

Brief

Brief in Support of Motion to Dismiss for Lack of Standing and Justiciability

▶ Key facts that may be important to our analysis:

▶ Constitutional Analysis:
  • Case:
    • Facts:

    • Holding:

    • Analysis:

  • Case:
    • Facts:

    • Holding:

    • Analysis:

▶ Standing of State Legislators to Bring Suit:
   In Favor:

   Against:

▶ Justiciability of Achivist's Actions:
   In Favor:

   Against:

CHAPTER THREE

Powers of Congress:
Commerce, Taxing, and Spending
Food Fight

IT'S MONDAY MORNING and Don, the head of your litigation work group, has called a war party. It seems that one of your client's legislative affairs people has gotten wind of new legislation that is being drafted and circulated among members of the House and Senate.

"Since the former First Lady was elected President," Don explains, "she is really pushing national legislation to combat what she terms 'the coming obesity catastrophe.' Congress is responding with unusual alacrity to her demand for 'action.' What we're hearing," he continues, "is that Congress wants to combat adult and childhood obesity by discouraging the production and sale of 'unhealthy foods.'"

Don circulates a single sheet of paper with bullet points printed on it. "This," he intones gravely, "doesn't leave this office. It is a copy of the provisions the chief sponsor wishes to see in the bill. Staffers and legislative aides will craft a bill. But reliable sources have told us that it will contain these elements."

The piece of paper reads:

INTERNAL MEMO
Not for Distribution

- No more than 20% of a food producer's total sales may come from sales of unhealthy food produced or sold in interstate or foreign commerce.

- "Unhealthy food" is defined as highly processed food high in refined sugar, fat, carbohydrates or calories.

- Producers who earn more than 20% from unhealthy food will be subject to an escalating "obesity mitigation fee" that begins at 5% of a company's net profit and rises to 15% of net profit.

- The money from the fee will be collected by the Department of Health and Human Services and made available to states for obesity reduction programs.

- To get the money, however, states must agree to pass laws restricting children's access to unhealthy food through, for example, limitations on size and quantities of unhealthy foods available for purchase, bans on vending machines from schools, and additional state taxes on unhealthy foods.

Attempting to stop obesity

— Not within ability of Congress

Don goes on to explain that FMA Foods is one of your firm's biggest, most profitable clients.

"As you know, the potato chips, nuts, and other snack foods that we all enjoy for free at the firm, are produced by FMA. I've been on the phone this morning with Mr. Keebler, the CEO. He is very concerned, and wants to explore his legal options should this legislation actually become law.

"FMA's net revenue for 2011 was $20 billion; and 50% of that revenue comes from sales of foods that could be deemed 'unhealthy' by the new law. This percentage would expose it to the top fee of 15% of net revenues, or $3 billion. Right now, FMA is focused on preventing this bill from ever seeing the light of day, but Mr. Keebler wants us ready to go in case we need to fight this out in court.

Don turns to you and says, "Therefore, what he wants from us is a letter, which he'll review with his in-house lawyers outlining possible challenges to this legislation and—assuming it contains the provisions on that sheet—our evaluation of the chances of success for each of the challenges. Address your letter to:

> Elvin Keebler
> FMA Foods
> 1 Donut Way
> Candyland, CA 10001."

As you head out the door, Don calls out, "Oh. Uh, one more thing. Keep careful track of your time. I'd swear that man has an army of elves that fly-speck our legal bills every month."

Later that day, over lunch, one of your friends at the firm mentions that the firm is negotiating a huge office lease for a new public interest group, the American Society for the Prevention of Obesity. She mentions that it has been a pain because the group demanded that vending machines in the building contain only healthy snacks and that no building in which it leased space had a food court lacking healthy eating choices. When you do an Internet search for the organization, you find a press release supporting the President's call for national legislation to curb unhealthy food consumption.

 Points to Consider:

(1) Can Congress ban the sales of a certain percentage of whatever it defines as unhealthy food? Could it ban the sale of *all* "unhealthy" food?

(1) What is Congress's authority for imposing the obesity mitigation fee? Is there more than one possible source of authority?

(2) How would you characterize the "fee"? Is it a "tax"?

(3) Can Congress condition receipt of money by the states on their agreeing to do certain things, like ban vending machines in schools? Are there limits to what Congress can require?

(4) Does the firm's representation of the American Society for the Prevention of Obesity present any conflicts? If so, how should they be addressed?

(5) Assume, too, that there is a history of diabetes runs in your family, that you are a committed vegan, and believe that companies like FMA produce very unhealthy food that harms a great number of people. May you ethically work on the case?

Client Letter

Your Law Firm, LLC
New York, Philadelphia, Wilmington

[Date]

Mr. Elvin Keebler
FMA Foods
1 Donut Way
Candyland, CA 10001.

Re:

Dear Mr. Keebler:

Client Letter, continued

Possible Challenges to Legislation:

Evaluation of Prospects for Success:

Sincerely,

Time Sheet

Attorney:

Client:

Billing No.

DATE	DESCRIPTION	TIME

The Dormant Commerce Clause Doctrine
Big Box Blues

ONE MONDAY MORNING you come in early after a long weekend. Among the hundreds of e-mail messages—you couldn't get a good signal on your smart phone in the mountains—one catches your eye. It's from your partner, Walker Roberts:

Re: Urgent: Need Analysis of Ordinance Quickly
Walker Roberts [wroberts@bigfirm.com]
To: Eager Young Associate [eya@bigfirm.com]

Sorry to dump this on you, but please see my assistant in the morning. She'll have a memo I just dictated with background material. I'm told you know a thing or two about constitutional law; this is one of those precious few times when that knowledge is actually useful!

I'm flying out this afternoon, and will be in meetings for the next couple of days, but let's get together when I get back.

— WR

On cue, Roberts's assistant shows up in your doorway holding a memo. As turns to leave, she says, "You know, I'm pretty sure that the firm represented Haul-Mart in a state tax controversy a couple of years ago.

I checked and found a copy of a bill marked 'PAID'. The file was closed, I think." Puzzled by her remark, you read the following memo.

MEMORANDUM

To: Eager Young Associate
From: Walker Roberts
Re: Proposed Size-Cap Ordinance

Our firm represents the town of Goodwish, Floribama, a small coastal town (pop. 5,000), composed of single family residences of 1,000 to 2,500 square feet in area and commercial businesses of 500 to 10,000 square feet in area. To date, Goodwish has not had any "big box" retail stores locate in the area. (If you haven't heard the term—it was new to me—big box stores offer a wide range of merchandise, either within a category (e.g., Home Depot, home building and repair; or Best Buy, electronic entertainment devices) or across a number of categories (e.g., Costco or Wal-Mart), in very large facilities (often several hundred thousand square feet in area), and usually featuring low prices.)

Big box stores are very large because they purchase in large quantities to obtain price discounts that are passed on to consumers. Because such stores reduce their profit margins, and thus undercut smaller competitors on price, they need large spaces to generate sufficient sales volume to make their business strategy profitable. But their size and the pressure they place on existing businesses have made them targets for local planning commissions and town councils.

The Goodwish town council learned that Haul-Mart, a large discount retailer and grocer incorporated and headquartered in a neighboring state, has purchased a vacant parcel of land, zoned for commercial use, on a highway on the outskirts of the town, but within the town limits, on which it is planning to construct a 250,000 square foot retail store. In response, the council is considering the attached ordinance, intended to limit the ability of Haul-Mart—or any other big box store—from opening stores in or around Goodwish. It will be considered at the next meeting; I persuaded them to let us give it a look before they acted on it.

I have some concerns that, as written, the ordinance violates the dormant Commerce Clause. I'd like you to take a look at it, assess it for constitutionality, and mark up the draft to correct any deficiencies you find by either adding language, striking some provisions, or both. In addition, I need you to draft a short memo explaining why you made any changes that you did. I'll want to review both before my meeting with the council. For purposes of your memo, you can assume that there's no federal legislation on the subject. I already checked on that.

—WR

Your partner has attached a copy of the Very Large Retail Store Ordinance. It reads as follows:

ORDINANCE
Town of Goodwish City Council

"The Goodwish Town Council makes the following findings of fact:

1. The town of Goodwish is a small town characterized by close personal relations among residents.

2. The character of Goodwish and the quality of life in Goodwish would be altered detrimentally by the destruction or erosion of those relationships.

3. The presence of very large retail stores, especially those that offer virtually every product within a given consumer category, located along major roads on the outskirts of Goodwish, will tend to increase traffic, promote development that is unfocused and sprawls, and contribute to degradation of the physical, social, and commercial environment of Goodwish.

Based on the foregoing, the Goodwish Town Council enacts into law the following:

1. No retail store may be established within the town of Goodwish if it occupies a floor area of 20,000 square feet or more, unless the owner shall have first obtained a Retail Special Use Permit from the Goodwish Town Council.

2. A Retail Special Use Permit shall be issued only if the applicant has established by clear and convincing evidence that the proposed retail store will not pose any appreciable threat to the factual premises upon which this Very Large Retail Store Ordinance is founded.

Points to Consider:

(1) Does the dormant Commerce Clause doctrine even apply here?

(2) Is there any evidence that the ordinance is discriminatory? Does that evidence appear anywhere in the ordinance?

(3) Would you recommend that the Council revise the ordinance to add any findings or operative provisions?

(4) Can the firm advise the Council on this matter? Using the form on the following page, draft a short email to Roberts explaining the situation and whether or not the Firm can act for the City in this matter.

Draft of Email

From:
To:
Cc:
Subject:

CHAPTER FIVE

Separation of Powers
Next Year in Jerusalem, Israel?

YOU ARE A LAWYER employed by the Department of Justice's Office of Legal Counsel, which acts as the main constitutional lawyers for the executive branch. Part of the OLC's duties involve scrutinizing recently-passed legislation for constitutionality and advising the President whether legislation is constitutional or not if there is some question. It also advises the President on the constitutionality of his actions as Chief Executive.

One morning, you get a text from your boss, the Assistant Attorney General:

> Come see me as soon as you get in

When you arrive at her office, hands you a thick piece of legislation with one provision highlighted.

"This," she explains, "is the recently-passed Foreign Relations Authorization Act. The highlighted provision, you'll notice, is entitled 'United States Policy with Respect to Jerusalem as the Capital of Israel.'"

You read the provision.

> § 214 **(d) RECORD OF PLACE OF BIRTH AS ISRAEL FOR PASSPORT PURPOSES**—For purposes of the registration of birth, certification of nationality, or issuance of a passport of a United States citizen born in the city of Jerusalem, the Secretary shall, upon the request of the citizen or the citizen's legal guardian, record the place of birth as Israel.

When you've finished, she continues, "The status of Jerusalem, and whether it is a part of Israel, is a hotly contested issue between Israelis and Palestinians. The executive branch wishes not to give offense or be seen as enlisting on either side of that debate, especially as it continues to seek a deal between Israelis and Palestinians that will bring peace to the Middle East. The executive branch reiterated that position publicly after the passage of § 214(d). That policy means that State Department officials are instructed that passports issued to U.S. citizens born in Jerusalem could not indicate 'Israel' as the place of birth."

She sounds like she's reading a press release, you think to yourself.

Your boss continues, "The President wishes to veto the legislation, or at least include a Presidential signing statement indicating that he will not enforce § 214(d) because it is an unconstitutional infringement of executive branch prerogatives. But you know the President, he also wants to have a firm legal basis for either vetoing the legislation or attaching the singing statement declining to enforce § 214(d). He has asked us to look at the issue. Characteristically, he wants two opinion letters prepared: one making the case that the provision *is* constitutional; the other, that it is unconstitutional. He'll decide what to do based on which one is the most persuasive. I need you to draft the opinion letter making the case that § 214(d) violates the Constitution. And I need it tomorrow."

Later that afternoon, while you're finishing your first draft, you receive a call from an acquaintance who works as a journalist for the *Washington Post*. "I'm doing a story on presidential signing statements and needed confirmation that the OLC prepares opinions for the President when he is considering making one," she says. "Can you confirm that your office is working on a legal opinion on this Jerusalem passport thing? I hear the President would like to avoid enforcing it."

"That's not quite true," you reply. "We're preparing two memos; he'll make his decision after he reads the pro and con memos."

After your friend hangs up, you are left with an uneasy feeling about the call that sticks with you the rest of the day.

 Points to Consider:

(1) How would you categorize the presidential-executive conflict under Justice Jackson's *Youngstown* opinion?

(2) What independent constitutional powers can the President point to in support of the argument that § 214(d) is unconstitutional? Are these *exclusive* powers?

(3) Are there other separation of powers arguments that the President could make in support of his position?

(4) Was your answer to the reporter improper or unethical?

Opinion Letter

United States Department of Justice
Office of the Assistant Attorney General

[Date]

To: The President of the United States
From: Your Name, Department of Justice, Legal Counsel's Office

Re: Enforcement of Foreign Relations Act § 214(d)

Sincerely,

Due Process Clause

Statehouse Standoff

RECENTLY, YOU WERE named chief legal counsel for the governor of your state after her election. She was a close friend in law school; though your paths diverged. You accepted a job at a law firm, she entered politics, but the two of you remained in touch. Her call to become her legal counsel surprised you, but at the time she said "I'm going to need someone who will give me good advice, isn't politically ambitious themselves, and won't hesitate to tell me when I'm wrong or doing something ill-advised."

Since taking the position, you've become a key part of her team, often offering much more than strictly legal advice. The press has deemed you the "vice-governor" and often you have to be very careful dealing with them, because it is assumed that you speak for the Governor.

The legislature she faces, however, is socially conservative, as are many of the voters in her state. The heads of the state house and senate have indicated support for legislation placing restrictions on abortion that would be among the strictest in the country.

According to the information she has, the following elements will be part of the law:

- A complete ban on post-viability abortions, except where necessary to save the life of the mother;

- Defining "viability" at 12 weeks

- Requirement of an abdominal ultrasound and counseling about the state of fetal development and about abortion alternatives

- A forty-eight hour waiting period

- Complete ban on the performance of abortions at any facility that receives state funding

The findings of the draft bill state that its purpose is to advance the interest of the state in protecting life and potential life. Moreover, they continue, it is the intent of the legislature to ensure that a woman's decision to terminate her pregnancy is "thoughtful and informed" and that she is given time to contemplate the gravity and irrevocability of the step as well as be advised of alternatives to aborting an unwanted child.

"This is bad," the Governor says. "I can't veto it because they'll just override me. I've counted the votes; I can't win."

"Well," you offer, "don't defend it if it's challenged."

"Yeah, they thought of that too. There's a special provision requiring the Attorney General to defend it. The worst part of it is that it's lawsuit bait. The state will be swarming with high priced lawyers seeking to challenge it and then seek attorney's fees under § 1983. I need your help."

"Sure. What do you want me to do?"

"Go to the leaders of the house and senate. Negotiate away some of the more obviously unconstitutional elements—this is the most restrictive law in the country, surely there is some low hanging fruit there. I never did like constitutional law, so I expect you'll know what they are. Make sure that whatever comes out of the house and senate can be upheld in court. And don't let them give you that whole *we're out to make new law* line. I don't think the Supreme Court is in the mood to revisit this issue and in any event I don't want our state to have to pay for the challenge!"

"Jeez. You don't ask for much."

"Give me something I can live with. And that the state can afford! I'm not going to sign it. I'll let it become law without my signature, but it needs to be something that can withstand challenge."

Points to Consider:

(1) Under current case law, which of the following elements
     are likely unconstitutional?

(2) Could any of those vulnerable provisions be modified to bring
     them within the permissible boundaries set by the Court?

(3) Most medical experts put fetal viability at around 24 weeks.
     Is the legislature bound by that finding? Can it otherwise
     define viability?

(4) What negotiating tactics might you employ to strengthen
     the Governor's hand?

(5) Can you tell the leaders that the Governor is absolutely opposed
     to negotiating and won't hesitate to veto the bill, even if you know
     that's not her position?

(6) Assume that you successfully negotiate a compromise bill with
     the legislatures. You leave government service and return to your
     firm. You are then approached by a partner who also heads the
     firm's pro bono efforts. He asks you to represent someone seeking
     to challenge the constitutionality of the new abortion law. Can you
     work on the matter? Can the firm?

> SUPPLEMENTAL: Negotiation Theory

There are two primary types of bargaining. In positional bargaining, the parties view the negotiation as a zero sum game where one party's gain is equivalent to the other party's loss. In interest-based bargaining, the parties view the negotiation as a problem-solving process rather than a zero-sum game. The parties are perceived to have complementary or mutual interests, so that bargaining may result in overall gains for both sides.

In positional bargaining, each party typically starts the negotiation from an extreme position (high or low rent, for example). The parties expect that small concessions gradually will be made by each side until a moderate or middle ground outcome is reached. Bluffing and puffing is common as the parties negotiate. When an attorney negotiates on behalf of a client, however, lying is prohibited as a violation of the lawyer's professional responsibilities under Rule 4.1 of the Model Rules of Professional Conduct.

Common strategies used in positional bargaining are:
  (1) make the other side offer first;
  (2) make the other side compromise first;
  (3) claim a lack of authority to do what the other side requests;
  (4) act irrationally; and
  (5) claim the other side is irrational or making unreasonable demands.

In interest-based bargaining, each party focuses on the problem to be solved and tries to identify at least one area of common interest where mutual gains may be achieved. Creative solutions are used to accommodate the goals and objectives of the parties.

Common strategies used in interest-based bargaining are:
  (1) focus on the problem, not the people or their personalities;
  (2) focus on the mutual interests of the parties, not on fixed demands or positions;
  (3) emphasize points of collaboration, not confrontation; and
  (4) empathize with the needs of the other side.

Depending on the circumstances, lawyers who are effective negotiators often use a combination of positional and interest-based bargaining to achieve the best result for their clients.

From: Colleen E. Medill, *Developing Professional Skills: Property* 47 (2012).

Notes in Preparation for Negotiation

Rules and Case Law:

1. Rules and case law governing whether this law is constitutional:

    a. Rule

    b. Case law

    c. Analysis of our facts

Possible Arguments:

1. Should the legislation be permitted?

    a. What will congressional leaders say?

    b. What is the Governor's position?

Notes for Negotiation, continued

Possible Points of Negotiation:

1. What are our points of compromise?

2. How can we strengthen the Governor's position?

Recommendations:

CHAPTER SEVEN

Equal Protection Clause
The Old College Try

LAST YEAR, one of your partners, Anita Flyte, was named university counsel to the flagship university, Ames University, in your State of Ames. Her appointment has been great for the firm, and for you personally, since you worked closely with Anita before her departure. You talk with her regularly and she frequently calls on the firm to assist her office in a wide variety of matters relating to the university. It's fascinating work involving everything from ensuring the university complies with due process in student conduct matters to intellectual property issues to personnel contracts. So it's no surprise when she asks you to meet with her and the University Provost at her office.

After a few minutes of small talk, she introduces you to Tracy Bloom, the Provost. Tracy, she explains, is representing the President of the University in your meeting. "When I came over," Anita begins, "the President asked me to take a look at the admissions department; specifically whether the formula used to determine admissions complied with the Supreme Court's decisions on race-based preferences."

"You see," Bloom interjects, "when the President took over a few years ago, he sought to cement this university's status as the flagship university for the whole system. He wanted to up the admissions standards, shrink the undergraduate population, and create a nationally-known honors program. We did this, but at a cost. You see, we began to see a real drop off in minority admissions and enrollment. Many of the minority students end up admitted to and enrolling at Ames State University, down the road. That began to create problems with our alums and, just as important, with the legislature. So, we tasked the Director of Admissions to remedy this.

"Remedy it he did, and our numbers jumped. In fact, they came up a little too quickly. Moreover, there was a somewhat disturbing correlation between the percentage of applicants, the percentage of enrollees, and the percentage of various minority groups in the state itself. I asked Anita here to review the processes, and, alas, we found out that the methods being used were, uh, questionable."

"Essentially," Anita continued, "the admissions office was running two separate admissions programs. In order to keep the averages up, only the highest scoring non-minority applicants were admitted. Minority applicants, on the other hand, were treated differently. I wasn't comfortable with the program and recommended that the admissions director be let go and the office restaffed."

"Which leaves the President with a problem: we can't have minority enrollment plummet again, but the President does not want to court a lawsuit. He has asked Anita to come up with guidelines for a new admissions diversity initiative that complies with applicable laws. We have some of his thoughts here," Bloom slides across a piece of paper entitled "Criteria Governing AU Admissions Diversity Initiative." On it are the following bullet points:

- Maintain as admissions goal acquisition of critical mass of underrepresented minority students (African-American, Latino/Native American) in order to further institutional interest in educational diversity

- Try to create a student body that looks like the State of Ames, e.g., has a similar racial make-up

- Also seek non-racial diversity (socio-economic status, life experience)

- Investigate possibility of race neutral means (automatic admission for top 10% of high school graduates in-state; 5% out-of-state) to increase diversity

- Maintain use of race as a "plus" factor if critical mass not projected to meet diversity goals

After you read them, Anita says, "The problem is that we've done some preliminary inquiries and though a race-neutral alternative could yield *some* racial diversity, it isn't comparable to what we had under the old admissions policy. We need to get together and frame some guidelines so that when the experts in the Admissions Office begin creating admissions criteria, we can keep them on the right side of the law."

"Can we count on courts to defer to our judgment?" asks Bloom. "That is, if we say that we've tried and can't reach 'critical mass' without using race, that is enough isn't it? I seem to remember that from the earlier cases in Michigan."

Anita says that you will work closely with her to devise some guide-lines for use by the Admissions Office when they flesh out the new admissions initiative. She asks you for a short memo outlining the limits of the use of race in light of the President's goals.

When you return to the office, you find an email from the firm's appellate practice group about a conflicts check for a brief they wish to file on behalf of a new client that will challenge race based preferences in federal court in a neighboring state.

Points to Consider:

(1) What standard of review governs the use of race in university admissions?

(2) If race-neutral alternatives are available, is the university obligated to exhaust them before using race?

(3) Who determines whether critical mass is met? Is that left to the university's judgment?

(4) Can you "stack" the use of race on top of a race neutral method to achieve critical mass?

(5) Can the law firm represent both the university and the client wishing to challenge racial preferences elsewhere?

Client Counseling Memorandum

Your Name:

Client Name:

Name of Client Representative:

Date:

Client goals:

Key points to be discussed:

Recommendations:

CHAPTER EIGHT

First Amendment—Free Speech 1

Living by the Sword

AFTER ENDURING THREE years of law school and an uncertain job market, you landed your dream job. You are a relatively new associate at Strunk & White, a boutique criminal defense firm specializing in white-collar crimes and other high-profile criminal matters. The hours are long and the work demanding, but it is never dull. You've been fortunate enough to be selected by Coleman Parker, a legendary litigator and counselor, to work closely with him. To your delight, you quickly learned that he intended to mentor you and so involved you in all of his major cases. Unfortunately, this means even more work. But you never knew who you would meet when he calls you into his office.

Not even pausing to grab a pad of paper, you hurry in. Sitting across from Parker is a trim man, in his late 50s or early 60s, very well dressed. But he looks like he hasn't slept. You notice he has bags under his eyes and he's missed a couple of spots shaving that morning. There's something familiar about him, but you can't put your finger on it. Parker pushes a legal pad and a pen across his desk to you. "Meet Jerry Miller. Mr. Miller, this is one of my associates."

Of course, you think. Jerry Miller is the head of DiamondPoint Capital Partners, one of the most successful hedge funds going. And apparently he's one of the richest folks in the country.

"Jerry," Parker says gently, "I know that this is difficult, but could you start over? I want to make sure we have all the information down so we can figure out what to do."

Miller sighs deeply. "As I was telling Coleman, my son Jay is in some trouble. But before I get to that, I have to tell you a little bit about him. About us." A pause. "I don't suppose that it will come as a surprise to you that being successful is not always compatible with being a good father or husband. There are late hours, stress, weekends and holidays foregone. I'm not excusing it, mind you. Like good lawyers, good money managers are service providers. Sometimes our clients must come first. Anyway, my son was always understanding. He looked up to me. He'd say, 'I want to be like you.' It was like that Harry Chapin song.

"I overcompensated by providing him whatever he wanted. He was a sweet boy, but a little directionless. I remember him asking me, 'What does it all mean?' I didn't know what to say. I'm not a religious man; I regarded those questions as above my pay grade. I just never thought about them. I suppose I should have listened more carefully.

"When Jay went to college, he did pretty well, but apparently he read too much Hunter Thompson or maybe William Blake. Who knows? He started drinking and using drugs. He got in a little trouble with the college, put on social probation. Coleman here," he nods toward Parker, "helped me out then. Funny thing is that Jay's grades slipped a little, but not much. So when he came to me after his sophomore year and said he was quitting college, I was completely flabbergasted. I'm telling you this, because it's important that you know he wasn't a stereotypical over-privileged kid taking a journey of self-discovery because no respectable college would have him."

"At first, I thought it might be great for him to take some time off. Figure out what he wanted out of life. His grandparents had left him some money; he didn't even need mine, really. He traveled to western

Europe at first, then North Africa, the Middle East. Somewhere along the way he picked up Arabic. He always had a thing for languages. For a while he sent emails. He said his travels had awakened a desire to live simply, honorably, justly. I thought he was going to come back and tell me he was going into the military, or the ministry," Miller says with a short barking laugh. "He sort of did both, in the end."

"Three years ago, Jay came back to the states. Before he returned, he sent a final email announcing that he had converted to Islam. He said he intended to follow the path of the Prophet, and no longer wished to have contact with me or the rest of the family. After that: nothing. Jay sort of dropped off the grid. He cleaned out his trust and bank accounts, ditched his phone, and began moving around frequently."

"Yesterday afternoon, I got a visit from the FBI at my office. At first, I thought they were investigating some sort of insider trading thing, but asked about Jay, and whether I knew where he was. I said I hadn't heard from him in a few years. Then one of them showed me a website called 'The Sword of Allah,' which they said Jay ran. Except now he calls himself 'Abdul al-Amriki.' A lot of it was typical *jihadi* nonsense— you know, the need for all devout Muslims to rise against the Zionists and their American enablers, calls for the restoration of the caliphate, that sort of thing. That surprised me: Jay was never like that, even when he began talking about converting to Islam. The FBI said they found comments Jay had posted at other websites, that I didn't even know existed, showing video of terrorist attacks, beheadings, really awful stuff. They said he praised the 'brothers' who had either martyred themselves or exacted revenge on the 'infidels.'

"Finally, they showed me a post from two days ago where they allege that Jay called for the death of the idiot preacher who insists on public burnings of the Qur'an and pictures of the Prophet Muhammad. His post was about the need of the righteous to bathe in the blood of the infidel, and that he hoped some of the 'righteous brothers' would make the pastor pay for his blasphemy. He even sent an email to the preacher saying that he would never 'escape the Sword of Allah' for his blasphemy. The feds found that among a number of emails that one might characterize as 'threatening'."

Your boss interrupts. "The day after that email was sent, the preacher and his wife were found murdered. Their throats were slit," he says. "A few things were missing, but the FBI doesn't think it was a robbery. While they don't think that Mr. Miller's son had anything directly to do with the murders, they've charged him with making threats and have suggested they might charge him with contributing material support to a terrorist organization. They have him in custody. In addition," Parker adds, "the state where they found Jay wants to charge him with incitement to commit violence, which is a felony."

Miller sighs. "I don't want my son to go to prison. It would kill him, and me. Please do whatever you can to keep him out. He didn't commit any of these acts; I'm not sure he even really has a sense of what it means to call for *jihad* and the like. I've no doubt he sincerely believes these things, but they can't put him in prison for that, can they?" Miller looks at you both pleadingly, then drops his shoulders, and sighs again. "He doesn't have to talk to me, all I ask is that you keep me in the loop and let me know he's going to be okay."

After an awkward silence, Parker says, "Jerry, we'll do everything we can. Try not to worry. We're going to talk about things and I'll give you a call this evening."

Miller leaves, closing the door behind him. As soon as the door clicks, you ask, "Have we even talked to Jay, uh . . . Abdul?" Parker waves your question aside, "First things first. Take a look at the email that the feds found, then take a look at both 18 U.S.C. 875(c) and the state incitement statute; I put both in the case file. From what he told us, I think we have a good First Amendment defense to both. I want you to lay out a First Amendment argument we can use to attempt to quash indictments on both charges. Be sure to note any facts that we might have to uncover to strengthen our case."

The two statutes read as follows:

---

18 USC 875(c):

Whoever transmits in interstate or foreign commerce any communication containing . . . any threat to injure the person of another, shall be fined under this title or imprisoned not more than five years, or both.

STATE INCITEMENT STATUTE:

(A) No person shall knowingly engage in conduct designed to urge or incite another to commit any offense of violence, when either of the following apply:
  (1) The conduct takes place under circumstances that create a clear and present danger that any offense of violence will be committed;
  (2) The conduct proximately results in the commission of any offense of violence.

The email from Miller to the preacher reads, in relevant part,

The Sword of the Prophet is swift and sure. Your only hope is to repent of your blasphemy and follow in the way of the one True Prophet. If not; if you continue your desecration of the One, bless his name, then you will not escape the Sword of Allah. You and the other unbelieving infidels will be struck down and the true believers will bathe in your blood. Allahu Akbar!

Points to Consider:

(1) Does Jay's email rise to the level of a "true threat" under current Supreme Court doctrine?

(2) Can Jay be prosecuted for "incitement" under current doctrine?

(3) What do you have to do in order to represent Jay Miller?
How much can you tell Mr. Miller during the representation?

Outline of Arguments to Dismiss Indictment

United States v. Miller

▶ Key First Amendment facts that may be important to our analysis:

▶ Constitutional Analysis:
- Case:
  - Facts:

  - Holding:

  - Analysis:

- Case:
  - Facts:

  - Holding:

  - Analysis:

Outline of Arguments, continued

▶ Arguments that indictment does not meet standards laid out in the state and federal statutes:

•*18 USC 875(c):*

•*State Incitement Statute:*

▶ Difficulties we may face in seeking dismissal of charges:

CHAPTER NINE

First Amendment—Free Speech 2
Soul Patrol

"GREAT," YOU RECALL thinking later, "just what I needed."
Earlier that morning, you received a somewhat panicked phone call
from the Superintendent of the Ames City Schools. One of your clients
is the Ames City School System.

"We might have a problem," he confides. "Can we meet later?
I'm bringing some people with me." Within an hour, you are seated
around a conference table with Richard Honer, Superintendent of the
Ames City Schools and two other people that you don't know.
Richard introduces them as Paula Evans, the principal at Ames High
School and Derek Lattimore, the Assistant Principal.

"Derek, why don't you start us off," says Richard.

Clearing his throat and sounding strangely as if he had rehearsed
this statement, Derek begins.

"About a year or two ago, in response to some bullying of students
who self-identify as gay, lesbian, or bisexual, Ames High School
permitted those GLB students to create a support group called 'OUT,'
which stands for 'Openness, Understanding, and Tolerance. Once a
year, OUT sponsors 'Pride Day,' during which they wear T-shirts and

buttons celebrating their decision to embrace their sexual identity and declare it openly. OUT members also sponsor a bake sale to raise money for the club." Here, he pauses, and looks at the Principal, who nods for him to continue.

"Okay, uh, anyway, there's this student, Paul."

"Paul Zonderman," the Principal adds.

"Oh, yeah, Paul Zonderman," Derek repeats. "Anyway, he's apparently a very devout Christian. He's active in several of the before-school Bible clubs that meet at the school and is, you know, very *vocal* about his beliefs. He's a bright kid, but one who is not afraid to, um, give his testimony. A student complained that Paul saw him reading Richard Dawkin's *The God Delusion* and wanted to engage in a debate with him. Then said he would pray for him."

"Derek," Richard interrupts, "let's talk about what happened last week."

"Sure. So, this year, on Pride Day, which was last week, Paul came to school in a T-shirt whose front had the words 'PRIDE DAY' in a red circle with a red line drawn diagonally through the words. On the back, the T-shirt read: 'HOMOSEXUALITY = ETERNAL DAMNATION.' Below those words, the shirt read, 'REPENT SINNERS, SAVE YOUR SOULS.'

"In addition, Paul approached some members of OUT to share his views with them before school and during lunch. One or two students debated Paul; others made it clear they didn't want to talk to him. Paul left those students alone. One of the students whom Paul approached complained to me that Paul was 'harassing' OUT members and was wearing an offensive and homophobic T-shirt."

Principal Evans then chimed in. "Derek came to me with the student's complaint about Paul. We were discussing it in the office when a teacher who happened to be in there too said that her students were talking about Paul's t-shirt and the conversations between him and members of OUT before class began.

"After lunch," she continued, "Derek and I called Paul in, told him of the complaints, and instructed him not to approach any member of OUT for the remainder of Pride Day. I also asked him to remove his T-shirt or cover it up," she pauses.

"What was his reaction," you ask, taking advantage of the lull.

"Well, the thing is, Paul sincerely believes that the GLB students' souls are in mortal peril. He said that he was trying to help them. So I read him our disruption and harassment policies."

She hands you a photocopied page from the Ames High School Student Handbook. It reads:

> *Any student who, during school hours, engages in behavior causing a substantial disruption to the school or whose behavior interferes with the rights of other students is subject to discipline including, but not limited to, detention, in-school suspension, out-of-school suspension, and expulsion.*

Another page of the Handbook subjects to similar discipline students who "harass" other students, faculty, or employees. "Harassment" is defined as "speech or conduct directed by one student towards another student, faculty member, or school employee that threatens, alarms, offends, or annoys that student, faculty member, or school employee."

Principal Evans continues. "After discussion with Derek, I told Paul that, in our opinion, his approach of the complaining student was harassment. His shirt and his actions were disruptive to the student and to the school generally; and his shirt violated the dress code because of the profanity it contained. I told him teachers had complained that their students couldn't stop talking about his shirt and his showdown with OUT and that all the talk was disrupting their classes."

"And what did Paul do then?" you prompt.

"Paul declined to remove his T-shirt or stop trying to, as he put it, save his fellow students' souls. So, I suspended him for a week. You see, the Handbook also requires students to comply with requests from administrators, faculty, and staff."

The Superintendent coughs slightly and says, "Yesterday, we received notice that Zonderman's parents hired an attorney and are demanding that we rescind the suspension and allow him to make up all work without penalty or they'll sue us in federal court. They're claiming that Principal Evans's actions violated Paul's free speech rights."

"Here's the thing," he continues, "I pride myself on backing my principals. I don't want to second-guess them or their staff when it comes to student discipline. But budgets are tight. I don't want to have to cancel women's soccer or the band's competition trips—because I've got to pay attorneys' fees if we lose, not to mention the legal bills we'd rack up ourselves. What I'd like from you is an honest assessment of whether we can successfully defend this in court, and a recommendation on a course of action. I'd like those recommendations even if you think we might prevail."

The meeting adjourns, but Superintendent Honer lingers after the other two have left. He closes the conference room door behind you. "We may have an additional problem. After we got the notice of suit,

Derek contacted me directly, asking to meet. He brought along a few emails to him from Principal Evans. Here's one of them, sent before Pride Day, about Paul's proselytizing":

> Derek—I am sick and tired of everyday being Paul Zonderman Day around here! He is a real pain in the a$$ with his God-squadding and I want you to do something about it. The next time you hear of him voicing an opinion about so much as what is being served for lunch, I want to know about it. With luck, he'll pull some stunt on Pride Day and we can have some peace around here for a few days. – Paula

The Superintendent moves towards the door. Over his shoulder he says, "I thought that might be relevant to your analysis," as he closes the door behind him.

No sooner has he left than you receive a page over the Firm's intercom. You take the call in the conference room. Principal Evans is on the other line, audibly upset.

"I really need your help. I, um, may have overreacted with Paul. I was upset. I was getting calls from parents—*influential* parents—who wanted me to 'do something.' Now I'm afraid that the Superintendent is going to throw me under the bus to save some money. What should I do? I need some advice. Can we meet a little later, just the two of us? All I've ever wanted to do was be a principal. I'd hate to lose that all now, over this."

Points to Consider:

(1) Which of Paul's actions constitution "speech"? The debates with members of OUT? The T-shirt?

(2) Under what circumstances, consistent with the First Amendment, can public schools punish students for the content of their speech?

(3) Which of Paul's actions violated which specific school policies? Are its policies consistent with student free speech rights the Court has recognized?

(4) Who is (are) your client(s)? Can you meet later with Principal Evans?

Client Counseling Memorandum

Your Name:

Client Name:

Name of Client Representative:

Date:

Client goals:

Key points to be discussed:

Recommendations:

CHAPTER TEN

First Amendment—Establishment and Free Exercise Clauses

Rotunda Rumble

THE SUPREME COURT of the State of Ames sits in an historic courthouse that dates from the mid-nineteenth century. Visitors, lawyers, and litigants walk up marble steps and enter massive bronze doors that open into a rotunda. Staircases on either side of the rotunda curve along the walls and lead upstairs to the actual Ames Supreme Court courtroom, where the Court sits and oral arguments are heard. There is an elevator located in the rotunda to provide the disabled with access to the courtroom.

Visitors to the rotunda (and the court) are confronted with a series of murals depicting the history of the State of Ames. On the far wall of the rotunda is an allegorical mural portraying early settlers to Ames being led by an angel out of the wilderness to a city on a hill by a river, which represents the early settlement of what would become Ames City. The settlers themselves carry an enormous, rough-hewn wooden cross. Several are shown in prayer as they exit the wilderness and see the spot toward which the angel is directing them. At the bottom, a caption reads "Settlers Give Thanks for God's Grace in Leading them to Ames City."

In addition to the historic courthouse, there is a newer administrative annex constructed two years ago because of space limitations in the old courthouse. The new annex is connected to the old courthouse through a narrow hallway. Lawyers and litigants regularly visit the annex to check schedules, file papers, and obtain information about their cases. The Ames Legislature requires a certain percentage of funds appropriated for public buildings to be spent acquiring original artwork from Ames artists. When the annex was constructed, the building committee commissioned a statue of Themis, the figure from Greek mythology who represents justice as a blindfolded woman holding scales and a sword. The statute now sits in the lobby of the new annex, in front of the information desk.

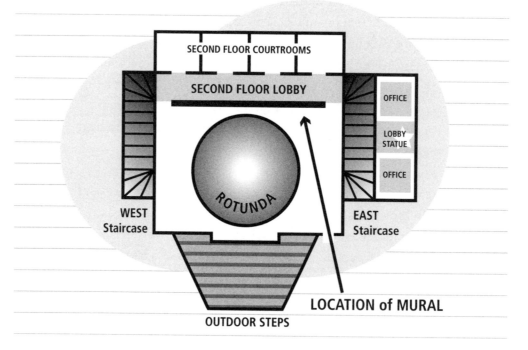

The year 1215 will mark the 800th anniversary of the signing of the Magna Carta. In celebration, a late thirteenth century copy owned by the U.S. government will tour state supreme courthouses for a year. In anticipation, the Chief Justice of the Ames Supreme Court,

Emily Reed, has created an educational display celebrating
"The Rule of Law and Pursuit of Justice in Western Civilization."
Copies of famous legal documents, along with placards explaining
their significance in the development of the rule of law, line the walls
by the dual staircases leading up to the second-floor courtroom.
The display begins with the Ten Commandments and excerpts from
the Torah, and ends at the top with the Ames State Constitution.
Other documents include the Mayflower Compact, the Declaration
of Independence, the U.S. Constitution, the Bill of Rights, the
Emancipation Proclamation, the Reconstruction Amendments, and
Franklin Roosevelt's "Four Freedoms." The placard accompanying
the Ten Commandments states that "the rule of law has roots in the
Judeo-Christian tradition of submission of individuals to law and
obedience to legitimate authority—a tradition that has endured as
the country has grown."

At a press conference during the unveiling of the display, the
Chief Justice said that she hoped the display would educate viewers
as to centrality of rule of law to Western civilization and would generate interest in visiting the courthouse when the Magna Carta was
on display as well.

You are a staff attorney with the Ames Civil Liberties Union.
Following the press conference, you get a call from Terry Barrow,
founder of the Ames Freethinkers Association, an atheist discussion
group dedicated to exposing organized religion as a fraud and a sham.
Barrow says that he has been approached by a number of lawyers,
litigants, and employees complaining about the planned display,
as well as about the existing murals. Barrow says that he would
like you represent the AFA's members and file suit seeking (1) the
removal or the veiling of the rotunda mural, and (2) the removal of the
display containing the Ten Commandments and the Torah from the
courthouse. Barrow claims that the mural and the display violate the
Establishment Clause. Excited at the prospect of bringing a constitu-

tional challenge, you promise Barrow you'll bring it up at your next office-wide meeting and get back to him.

Somewhat to your surprise at the meeting, the head of your office, Rich Baldwin, is apprehensive about the litigation.

"This kind of litigation garners us terrible press and, frankly, it hurts fundraising efforts," he says. "Further complicating things," he adds, "Chief Justice Reed has been very good on other First and Fourth Amendment issues. I'd hate to alienate her."

You begin to make an impassioned plea about principle and the Constitution when Baldwin cuts you off.

"I know. Some elements of the courthouse display strike me as more problematic than others. Why don't you contact the Chief Justice, indicate that we have some clients with concerns about the display and the mural and see if you can't negotiate some mutually acceptable resolution. With the state's finances in the shape they're in, I would suppose that they aren't anxious to litigate. If you can't get anywhere with them, well . . . let's just cross that bridge when we come to it."

A little discouraged, you head back to your office in time to catch the phone while it is still ringing. Your caller, Roy Duhr, says that he is also a lawyer and a devout Christian. He would like the Ames ACLU to represent him in a suit against the state seeking the removal of the statue of Themis from the annex lobby. Duhr claims that the display of the statue constitutes an establishment of a pagan religion on the part of the state. When you express some reluctance, he exclaims, "Just as I thought! Your say you're for separation of church and state, but you're not! You're just anti-Christian. Prove me wrong; take *my* case if you really are all about principle!"

 **Points to Consider:**

(1) What would you say to Barrow about your meeting with Baldwin?

(2) Which part or parts of the display is most vulnerable under current Supreme Court doctrine?

(3) Which are least vulnerable?

(4) What strategy would you adopt when negotiating with the Chief Justice?

(5) What would you tell Roy Duhr? Do agree to propose taking his case? What if your boss, Baldwin, upon hearing about Duhr's call, says, "Great! Take that and it could offset any bad publicity we might get suing over the display, if it comes to that."

Notes in Preparation for Negotiation

Rules and Case Law:

1. Rules and case law governing whether the display and mural are (or are not) protected under the First Amendment

    • Rule:

    • Case law:

    • Analysis of our facts:

    • Rule:

    • Case law:

    • Analysis of our facts:

Possible Considerations:

1. Which parts of the display are most vulnerable to challenge under the Establishment Clause ? Which are least vulnerable?

Possible Points of Negotiation:

Negotiation Strategies:

Recommendations:

APPENDIX A
Selected Provisions of the Model Rules
of Professional Conduct

Rule 1.0 Terminology

(a) "Belief" or "believes" denotes that the person involved actually supposed the fact in question to be true. A person's belief may be inferred from circumstances.

(b) "Confirmed in writing," when used in reference to the informed consent of a person, denotes informed consent that is given in writing by the person or a writing that a lawyer promptly transmits to the person confirming an oral informed consent. See paragraph (e) for the definition of "informed consent." If it is not feasible to obtain or transmit

the writing at the time the person gives informed consent,
then the lawyer must obtain or transmit it within a reasonable
time thereafter.

(c) "Firm" or "law firm" denotes a lawyer or lawyers in a law partnership, professional corporation, sole proprietorship or other association authorized to practice law; or lawyers employed in a legal
services organization or the legal department of a corporation or
other organization.

(d) "Fraud" or "fraudulent" denotes conduct that is fraudulent under
the substantive or procedural law of the applicable jurisdiction and
has a purpose to deceive.

(e) "Informed consent" denotes the agreement by a person to a proposed course of conduct after the lawyer has communicated adequate information and explanation about the material risks of and
reasonably available alternatives to the proposed course of conduct.

(f) "Knowingly," "known," or "knows" denotes actual knowledge of
the fact in question. A person's knowledge may be inferred from
circumstances.

(g) "Partner" denotes a member of a partnership, a shareholder in a
law firm organized as a professional corporation, or a member of an
association authorized to practice law.

(h) Reasonable" or "reasonably" when used in relation to conduct
by a lawyer denotes the conduct of a reasonably prudent and
competent lawyer.

(i) "Reasonable belief" or "reasonably believes" when used in
reference to a lawyer denotes that the lawyer believes the matter in
question and that the circumstances are such that the belief
is reasonable.

(j) "Reasonably should know" when used in reference to a lawyer denotes that a lawyer of reasonable prudence and competence would ascertain the matter in question.

(k) "Screened" denotes the isolation of a lawyer from any participation in a matter through the timely imposition of procedures within a firm that are reasonably adequate under the circumstances to protect information that the isolated lawyer is obligated to protect under the Rules or other law.

(l) "Substantial" when used in reference to degree or extent denotes a material matter of clear and weighty importance.

(m) "Tribunal" denotes a court, an arbitrator in a binding arbitration proceeding or a legislative body, administrative agency or other body acting in an adjudicative capacity. A legislative body, administrative agency or other body acts in an adjudicative capacity when a neutral official, after the presentation of evidence or legal argument by a party or parties, will render a binding legal judgment directly affecting a party's interests in a particular matter.

(n) "Writing" or "written" denotes a tangible or electronic record of a communication or representation, including handwriting, typewriting, printing, photostatting, photography, audio or video-recording, and electronic communications. A "signed" writing includes an electronic sound, symbol or process attached to or logically associated with a writing and executed or adopted by a person with the intent to sign the writing.

Rule 1.1 Competence

A lawyer shall provide competent representation to a client. Competent representation requires the legal knowledge, skill, thoroughness and preparation reasonably necessary for the representation.

Rule 1.2 Scope of Representation And Allocation of Authority Between Client and Lawyer

(a) Subject to paragraph (c) and (d), a lawyer shall abide by a client's decisions concerning the objectives of representation and, as required by Rule 1.4, shall consult with the client as to the means by which they are to be pursued. A lawyer may take such action on behalf of the client as is impliedly authorized to carry out the representation. A lawyer shall abide by a client's decision whether to settle a matter...

(b) A lawyer's representation of a client, including representation by appointment, does not constitute an endorsement of the client's political, economic, social or moral views or activities.

(c) A lawyer may limit the scope of the representation if the limitation is reasonable under the circumstances and the client gives informed consent.

(d) A lawyer shall not counsel a client to engage, or assist a client, in conduct that the lawyer knows is criminal or fraudulent, but a lawyer may discuss the legal consequences of any proposed course of conduct with a client and may counsel or assist a client to make a good faith effort to determine the validity, scope, meaning or application of the law.

Rule 1.4 Communication

(a) A lawyer shall:

    (1) promptly inform the client of any decision or circumstance with respect to which the client's informed consent, as defined in Rule 1.0(e), is required by these Rules;

    (2) reasonably consult with the client about the means by which the client's objectives are to be accomplished;

    (3) keep the client reasonably informed about the status of the matter;

(4) promptly comply with reasonably requests for information; and

(5) consult with the client about any relevant limitation on the lawyer's conduct when the lawyer knows that the client expects assistance not permitted by the Rules of Professional Conduct or other law.

(b) A lawyer shall explain a matter to the extent reasonably necessary to permit the client to make informed decisions regarding the representation.

Rule 1.6 Confidentiality of Information

(a) A lawyer shall not reveal information relating to the representation of a client unless the client gives informed consent, the disclosure is impliedly authorized in order to carry out the representation or the disclosure is permitted by paragraph (b).

(b) A lawyer may reveal information relating to the representation of a client to the extent the lawyer reasonably believes necessary:

(1) to prevent reasonably certain death or substantial bodily harm;

(2) to prevent the client from committing a crime or fraud that is reasonably certain to result in substantial injury to the financial interests or property of another and in furtherance of which the client has used or is using the lawyer's services;

(3) to prevent, mitigate or rectify substantial injury to the financial interests or property or another that is reasonably certain to result or has resulted from the client's commission of a crime or fraud in furtherance of which the client has used the lawyer's services;

(4) to secure legal advice about the lawyer's compliance with these Rules;

(5) to establish a claim or defense on behalf of the lawyer in a controversy between the lawyer and the client, to establish a defense to a criminal charge or civil claim against the lawyer based upon conduct in which the client was involved, or to respond to allegations in any proceeding concerning the lawyer's representation of the client;

(6) to comply with other law or a court order; or

(7) to detect and resolve conflicts of interest arising from the lawyer's change of employment or from changes in the composition or ownership of a firm, but only if the revealed information would not compromise the attorney-client privilege or otherwise prejudice the client.

(c) A lawyer shall make reasonable efforts to prevent the inadvertent or unauthorized disclosure of, or unauthorized access to, information relating to the representation of a client.

Rule 1.7   Conflict of Interest: Current Clients

(a) Except as provided in paragraph (b), a lawyer shall not represent a client if the representation involves a concurrent conflict of interest.

A concurrent conflict of interest exists if:

(1) the representation of one client will be directly adverse to another client; or

(2) there is a significant risk that the representation of one or more clients will be materially limited by the lawyer's responsibilities to another client, a former client or a third person or by a personal interest of the lawyer.

(b) Notwithstanding the existence of a concurrent conflict of interest under paragraph (a), a lawyer may represent a client if:

(1) the lawyer reasonably believes that the lawyer will be able to provide competent and diligent representation to each affected client;

(2) the representation is not prohibited by law;

(3) the representation does not involve the assertion of a claim by one client against another client represented by the lawyer in the same litigation or other proceeding before a tribunal; and

(4) each affected client gives informed consent, confirmed in writing.

Rule 1.9 Duties to Former Clients

(a) A lawyer who has formerly represented a client in a matter shall not thereafter represent another person in the same or a substantially related matter in which that person's interests are materially adverse to the interests of the former client unless the former client gives informed consent, confirmed in writing.

(b) A lawyer shall not knowingly represent a person in the same or a substantially related matter in which a firm with which the lawyer formerly was associated had previously represented a client

(1) whose interests are materially adverse to that person; and

(2) about whom the lawyer had acquired information protected by Rules 1.6 and 1.9(c) that is material to the matter; unless the former client gives informed consent, confirmed in writing.

(c) A lawyer who has formerly represented a client in a matter or whose present or former firm has formerly represented a client in a matter shall not thereafter:

(1) use information relating to the representation to the disadvantage of the former client except as these Rules would permit or require with respect to a client, or when the information has become generally known; or

(2) reveal information relating to the representation except as these Rules would permit or require with respect to a client.

Rule 1.10: Imputation of Conflicts of Interest: General Rule

(a) While lawyers are associated in a firm, none of them shall knowingly represent a client when any one of them practicing alone would be prohibited from doing so by Rules 1.7 or 1.9, unless

(1) the prohibition is based on a personal interest of the disqualified lawyer and does not present a significant risk of materially limiting the representation of the client by the remaining lawyers in the firm; or

(2) the prohibition is based upon Rule 1.9(a) or (b) and arises out of the disqualified lawyer's association with a prior firm, and

(i) the disqualified lawyer is timely screened from any participation in the matter and is apportioned no part of the fee therefrom;

(ii) written notice is promptly given to any affected former client to enable the former client to ascertain compliance with the provisions of this Rule, which shall include a description of the screening procedures employed; a statement of the firm's and of the screened lawyer's compliance with these Rules; a statement that review may be available before a tribunal; and an agreement by the firm to respond promptly to any written inquiries or objections by the former client about the screening procedures; and

(iii) certifications of compliance with these Rules and with the screening procedures are provided to the former client by the screened lawyer and by a partner of the firm, at reasonable intervals upon the former client's written request and upon termination of the screening procedures.

(b) When a lawyer has terminated an association with a firm, the firm is not prohibited from thereafter representing a person with interests materially adverse to those of a client represented by the formerly associated lawyer and not currently represented by the firm, unless:

    (1) the matter is the same or substantially related to that in which the formerly associated lawyer represented the client; and

    (2) any lawyer remaining in the firm has information protected by Rules 1.6 and 1.9(c) that is material to the matter.

(c) A disqualification prescribed by this rule may be waived by the affected client under the conditions stated in Rule 1.7.

(d) The disqualification of lawyers associated in a firm with former or current government lawyers is governed by Rule 1.11.

Rule 1.11 Special Conflicts Of Interest for Former and Current Government Officers And Employees

(a) Except as law may otherwise expressly permit, a lawyer who has formerly served as a public officer or employee of the government:

    (1) is subject to Rule 1.9(c); and

    (2) shall not otherwise represent a client in connection with a matter in which the lawyer participated personally and substantially as a public officer or employee, unless the appropriate government agency gives its informed consent, confirmed in writing, to the representation.

(b) When a lawyer is disqualified from representation under paragraph (a), no lawyer in a firm with which that lawyer is associated may knowingly undertake or continue representation in such a matter unless:

(1) the disqualified lawyer is timely screened from any participation in the matter and is apportioned no part of the fee therefrom; and

(2) written notice is promptly given to the appropriate government agency to enable it to ascertain compliance with the provisions of this rule.

(c) Except as law may otherwise expressly permit, a lawyer having information that the lawyer knows is confidential government information about a person acquired when the lawyer was a public officer or employee, may not represent a private client whose interests are adverse to that person in a matter in which the information could be used to the material disadvantage of that person. As used in this Rule, the term "confidential government information" means information that has been obtained under governmental authority and which, at the time this Rule is applied, the government is prohibited by law from disclosing to the public or has a legal privilege not to disclose and which is not otherwise available to the public. A firm with which that lawyer is associated may undertake or continue representation in the matter only if the disqualified lawyer is timely screened from any participation in the matter and is apportioned no part of the fee therefrom.

(d) Except as law may otherwise expressly permit, a lawyer currently serving as a public officer or employee:

(1) is subject to Rules 1.7 and 1.9; and
(2) shall not:
(i) participate in a matter in which the lawyer participated personally and substantially while in private practice or nongovernmental employment, unless the appropriate government agency gives its informed consent, confirmed in writing; or
(ii) negotiate for private employment with any person who is involved as a party or as lawyer for a party in a matter in

which the lawyer is participating personally and substantially, except that a lawyer serving as a law clerk to a judge, other adjudicative officer or arbitrator may negotiate for private employment as permitted by Rule 1.12(b) and subject to the conditions stated in Rule 1.12(b).

(e) As used in this Rule, the term "matter" includes:

(1) any judicial or other proceeding, application, request for a ruling or other determination, contract, claim, controversy, investigation, charge, accusation, arrest or other particular matter involving a specific party or parties, and

2) any other matter covered by the conflict of interest rules of the appropriate government agency.

Rule 1.13 Organization as Client

(a) A lawyer employed or retained by an organization represents the organization acting through its duly authorized constituents.

(b) If a lawyer for an organization knows that an officer, employee or other person associated with the organization is engaged in action, intends to act or refuses to act in a matter related to the representation that is a violation of a legal obligation to the organization, or a violation of law that reasonably might be imputed to the organization, and that is likely to result in substantial injury to the organization, then the lawyer shall proceed as is reasonably necessary in the best interest of the organization. Unless the lawyer reasonably believes that it is not necessary in the best interest of the organization to do so, the lawyer shall refer the matter to higher authority in the organization, including, if warranted by the circumstances to the highest authority that can act on behalf of the organization as determined by applicable law.

(c) Except as provided in paragraph (d), if:

    (1) despite the lawyer's effort in accordance with paragraph (b) the highest authority that can act on behalf of the organization insists upon or fails to address in a timely and appropriate manner an action, or a refusal to act, that is clearly a violation of law, and

    (2) the lawyer reasonably believes that the violation is reasonably certain to result in substantial injury to the organization, then the lawyer may reveal information relating to the representation whether or not Rule 1.6 permits such disclosure, but only if and to the extent the lawyer reasonably believes necessary to prevent substantial injury to the organization.

(d) Paragraph (c) shall not apply with respect to information relating to a lawyer's representation of an organization to investigate an alleged violation of law, or to defend the organization or an officer, employee or other constituent associated with the organization against a claim arising out of an alleged violation of law.

(e) A lawyer who reasonably believes that he or she has been discharged because of the lawyer's actions taken pursuant to paragraphs (b) or (c), or who withdraws under circumstances that require or permit the lawyer to take action under either of those paragraphs, shall proceed as the lawyer reasonably believes necessary to assure that the organization's highest authority is informed of the lawyer's discharge or withdrawal.

(f) In dealing with an organization's directors, officers, employees, members, shareholders or other constituents, a lawyer shall explain the identity of the client when the lawyer knows or reasonably should know that the organization's interests are adverse to those of the constituents with whom the lawyer is dealing.

(g) A lawyer representing an organization may also represent any of
its directors, officers, employees, members, shareholders or other
constituents, subject to the provisions of Rule 1.7. If the organization's consent to the dual representation is required by Rule 1.7,
the consent shall be given by an appropriate official of the organization other than the individual who is to be represented, or by
the shareholders.

Rule 1.16 Declining Or Terminating Representation

(a) Except as stated in paragraph (c), a lawyer shall not represent a
client or, where representation has commenced, shall withdraw
from the representation of a client if:

    (1) the representation will result in violation of the Rules of
Professional Conduct or other law;

    (2) the lawyer's physical or mental condition materially impairs
the lawyer's ability to represent the client; or

    (3) the lawyer is discharged.

(b) Except as stated in paragraph (c), a lawyer may withdraw from
representing a client if:

    (1) withdrawal can be accomplished without material adverse
effect on the interests of the client;

    (2) the client persists in a course of action involving the
lawyer's services that the lawyer reasonably believes is
criminal or fraudulent;

    (3) the client has used the lawyer's services to perpetrate a
crime or fraud;

    (4) the client insists upon taking action that the lawyer
considers repugnant or with which the lawyer has a
fundamental disagreement;

    (5) the client fails substantially to fulfill an obligation to the
lawyer regarding the lawyer's services and has been given
reasonable warning that the lawyer will withdraw unless
the obligation is fulfilled;

(6) the representation will result in an unreasonable financial burden on the lawyer or has been rendered unreasonably difficult by the client; or

(7) other good cause for withdrawal exists.

(c) A lawyer must comply with applicable law requiring notice to or permission of a tribunal when terminating a representation. When ordered to do so by a tribunal, a lawyer shall continue representation notwithstanding good cause for terminating the representation.

(d) Upon termination of representation, a lawyer shall take steps to the extent reasonably practicable to protect a client's interests, such as giving reasonable notice to the client, allowing time for employment of other counsel, surrendering papers and property to which the client is entitled and refunding any advance payment of fee or expense that has not been earned or incurred. The lawyer may retain papers relating to the client to the extent permitted by law.

Rule 2.1 Advisor

In representing a client, a lawyer shall exercise independent professional judgment and render candid advice. In rendering advice, a lawyer may refer not only to law but to other consideration such as moral, economic, social and political factors, that may be relevant to the client's situation.

Rule 4.1 Truthfulness In Statements to Others

In the course of representing a client a lawyer shall not knowingly:

(a) make a false statement of material fact or law to a third person; or

(b) fail to disclose a material fact to a third person when disclosure is necessary to avoid assisting a criminal or fraudulent act by a client, unless disclosure is prohibited by Rule 1.6.

Rule 4.3 Dealing With Unrepresented Person

In dealing on behalf of a client with a person who is not represented by counsel, a lawyer shall not state or imply that the lawyer is disinterested. When the lawyer knows or reasonably should know that the unrepresented person misunderstands the lawyer's role in the matter, the lawyer shall make reasonable efforts to correct the misunderstanding. The lawyer shall not give legal advice to an unrepresented person, other than the advice to secure counsel, if the lawyer knows or reasonably should know that the interests of such a person are or have a reasonable possibility of being in conflict with the interests of the client.

Time Sheet

Attorney:

Client:

Billing No.

DATE	DESCRIPTION	TIME

Time Sheet

Attorney:

Client:

Billing No.

DATE	DESCRIPTION	TIME

Time Sheet

Attorney:

Client:

Billing No.

DATE	DESCRIPTION	TIME

Time Sheet

Attorney:
Client:
Billing No.

DATE	DESCRIPTION	TIME

Time Sheet

Attorney:

Client:

Billing No.

DATE	DESCRIPTION	TIME

Time Sheet

Attorney:

Client:

Billing No.

DATE	DESCRIPTION	TIME

Time Sheet

Attorney:
Client:
Billing No.

DATE	DESCRIPTION	TIME

Time Sheet

Attorney:

Client:

Billing No.

DATE	DESCRIPTION	TIME